This book is dedicated to Jehovah who encouraged me to live past 70 years old and to publish this book, and the people he used. Besides the many influential persons in my life, I owe this renewed zest for life to you!

Jehovah, My God and Father, Is Real

W. Dwightel Weathers

PAGE PUBLISHING, INC.
New York, NY

First originally published by Page Publishing, Inc. 2019

ISBN 978-1-68456-696-9 (Paperback)
ISBN 978-1-68456-698-3 (Hardcover)
ISBN 978-1-68456-697-6 (Digital)

Printed in the United States of America

In these present days of my life, starting from the summer of 1972, Father Jehovah began to confirm his purpose for my life. Throughout the course of my life, he has been there, guiding me around the failures and the mischief of youth. He also protected *me* from deadly circumstances. In February 1973, he restored my life, and I called it being born again. After my rebirth, many things began happening in my life. I did receive power as Jesus had said his disciples would after the Holy Ghost (Spirit) came upon them. Along with the power came an enemy that I was not aware of. He tried to steer me away from the course Father set for me. For months, I struggled in captivity while my life was tried, and my union with Father and Jehoshua (Jesus) was tried. I was delivered from these trials and set free to go the way I should.

Though there were many who claimed faith and trust in the Messiah as the Christ, they did not know what I was experiencing. In fact, they had been taught and were teaching that what was happening to me was not supposed to happen. They prayed for me and with me, but they could not understand me. One said, "Can't do anything with him and can't do anything without him." This was after he had told me that I was not teaching what they were teaching and that if I couldn't teach what they were teaching about the Trinity, I couldn't teach. As I left the congregation, I asked Father if I had taught anything wrong, and he said, "No!" However, on the following Sunday, the pastor ripped me up, from the pulpit, in his message! After the service, I went to him and conceded that I could not teach. He asked if I had been talking to my uncle, and I replied, "No! I heard every word you said!" With a bowed head and a different voice, he said, "We need you to teach our children." So life went on. I finished college at Miami Dade Community College, worked a year in my dad's lawn business and as a security guard job until Dad was able to work again! Then I was off to college to finish my degree in Religious Studies at the University of West Florida, Pensacola, Florida.

Before I applied to the university, I applied at Hebrew University, Jerusalem, Israel, and was rejected! However, Tel Aviv University did accept me even though I did not apply there. I was set on Hebrew University and did not respond. So off to the University of West Florida I went. While at Miami Dade Community College, I met two lovely ladies. We're still friends to this day, and we were going to the university together until my dad had health issues. I went there as they were finishing, and they left. I joined a campus ministry named the Baptist Campus Ministry, sponsored by Marvin Howard and his wife, Kitty. We engaged in many *activities* together and since we were from *different* places in Florida, and some were outside Florida, we introduced ourselves. At one such introduction, a young lady identified herself, her major course of study, and said that she did not know why she came to the university.

Time passed, and we had many activities under our belts, including even a trip to Lake Wales, Florida, for a retreat. We were at her apartment for a farewell fellowship. Again, we all introduced ourselves, told our majors and why we came to the university. Again, she did not know, after all this time, why she came to the university. We had all bonded as good friends, and I had taken a special interest in bringing her into the group. And so, as we were leaving, I said to her that I would pray for her that Father would show her why she came to the university, and then I would pray with her for the same reason. I was the last to leave, and when I got into my car and began to leave, I began to pray for her, and immediately, a voice said, "She came to marry you!" I asked that he not be allowed to tell me that. The voice was masculine. At that point, I had only finished my bachelor's degree and had, at least, a masters to finish. In the past, when I engaged a girl in a relationship, things went well when we were on one accord, but when we were not and were having trouble, I could not study. My grades suffered, and I didn't want that anymore. So I rejected the idea. I did not consider who was talking and how powerful he is to accomplish whatever he wills. Also, I didn't think about the fact that we didn't have to get married right away. Anyway, I went home for the summer and worked with my dad and uncle, doing lawn work. I took care of expenses and spent just about every other cent on phone calls to her and our friends. My love for her intensified beyond my control. She was always happy to hear from me, and my friends were happy to share about her as well.

The summer was over. I returned for my last quarter at the university, and I met with her and another high school youth. We were driving when she asked me about marriage. I was shocked because I had not prayed with her, nor had I ever spoken with her about what the Spirit said. So I laughed! That didn't change the way I felt about her, but it discouraged her, I suppose. When I went off to seminary, she and others began trying to set me up with other ladies. She was the only one for me. But since she seemed not to want me, I became vulnerable to my own likes. I like fine, smart, and beautiful ladies who have grace, poise, and a talent for greatness, with long hair and a shapely body! At a funeral in Henderson, North Carolina, I saw such a woman. We were introduced because I was a friend of the deceased, and the widow of the deceased introduced us. She was married to a minister of the gospel. Therefore, any relationship with her was out of the question. However, she, her husband, and I became friends. He and I talked on the phone, but we never met face-to-face. He later died, and I called her to comfort and to console her. I also called the wife of the deceased. That precipitated our meeting for the same reason. But she began matchmaking the two of us. And we did get together and married. Father allowed our marriage, but we were not a good match, and we ended in separation and then divorce.

We discussed our separation, and I was given two weeks to find a place. I had no idea where I would go, but I went to church for Sunday school and worship. After the services and greetings, I was headed back down the hill, to our home, when an elderly lady asked me if I needed a place to stay. I said, yes! She offered me a room in her apartment, saying that she and her foster child were often away and that I would have my room and full run of the common space. What is odd about this is that neither my wife, nor I had told anyone about my situation. But Father knew, and he is very much active in our lives. I am up and writing this right now because of his guidance. Also, it was less than a day when this all happened between the elderly lady and me. Father is quick!

Decades have passed, and I have been married two more times. The second was to a high school alumnus! She graduated the year I should have, but due to some trials and tribulations in Mississippi, I graduated two years later than I should have. However, Father has always worked for my benefit. She and I lasted eighteen months before I realized that we would not make it to heaven together and that, even though we were (are) only days apart in age, we just don't fit. The last marriage was an arranged marriage that I consented to before consulting Father about it. After giving my word, I thought and went to him for approval and guidance. He said, "I wish you had asked me first! Your word is all that you have! If your word is true, then you are true! If you are not the truth, then you are a lie! You can marry her, but do not touch her!"

After our arrangement was completed and she had her legal documents, she left. She told me where she was going, but I don't like the cold and I was not going. She called me for my birthday in 2002, and since I was in worship, she left a message. She didn't answer when I returned her call, and she never called back. Sometime later, Father told me to divorce her. I heard him clearly, but I had done this divorce thing two times before and was embarrassed to do it again. But one November day in 2015, I met a young lady who changed my life and opened the door for the love of my life! She was not the one who should be the love of my life. Yet I love her and remember her until I cannot because, without her being available to Father, I had not met the next two ladies and the last love of my life! I will never forget the second lady either! She stirred in me what I thought was dead and when I thought that my life on earth would soon be over. But she, a young, beautiful, and voluptuous young woman, wanted to marry me. We inquired about our age, and we were too far apart! She was twenty-nine, and I was sixty-nine. I told her that she was too young. I liked her though! And I would come to the mall to see her! She brought another young lady with her the next time I saw her.

I believe it was the next time. Anyway, as we talked, randomly, the other young lady blurted out, "And you're too young for me!" I was totally shocked. I realized that I was a topic of conversation among these young people, ladies especially!

I asked, "What is old enough for you?"

She replied, "Seventy-two!"

"How old are you?" I asked. Thirty-two was her answer.

Although she was very beautiful and has a great voice, she was too small for me, and of course, I was too young for her! I considered that the young lady was serious about marrying me. So I went to the court to get proof of my divorce from my two Florida wives. Only one was complete. I went to the clerk for marriage licensing and got a copy of the marriage license then went to see about getting divorced from my wife from the arranged marriage. The clerk who sold the divorce package sold me the wrong package and discouraged me by telling me it would take six months for it to be final. But I started the process anyway. I finally got it completed and went to the clerk for the next step. The clerk, a lady, told me I had the wrong papers and gave me the right ones and told me to fill them out and come back. I went back, and this time, I saw a man, and everything went smoothly. However, it was much too late for the young lady who encouraged me to get on with the process, as well as for my current love!

Father made me to love her exclusively and also advised me to purchase skin-care products from her alone. One day, she left the mall, and I would buy from her at home! She and her boss continued to me the charade that they were lovers. I would never bother her with being anything but my friend and skin-care salesperson. But one day, I got the courage to ask to see her, at the urging of the Spirit of Father, to go out with me. She said that she couldn't see me anymore because she was leaving. Through text, I begged her to let me see her and told her that it was urgent. She wanted to know why, and though I didn't want to do it that way, I asked her to marry me! She asked me why, and I said it was to fulfill all that Father wanted us to do! And I felt that my life would surely end if she left! And though I am still alive and breathing and chatting with her from time to time, even yesterday, I am not as alive as I would be with her!

Today, she is living back in Israel and vacationing over the world with friends and family. She is my second God-given wife-to-be, and this time, except for being slow, I am trying not to mess up our jives. I pray Father will keep us for each other, and thus, fulfill his course for our lives so that it may end in joy and success and I may leave this body as Father would have me come to him! Twenty years before she was born, Father showed her to me in a dream/vision and, ten days later, gave me a poetic description of her! She was another young lady, but she was completely raptured with the person of Jesus (Jehoshua)! I love her as I can love no other. Because she is away, some feel that I can and should go out with others. Others tell me that I should move on. In either case, I have no desire for anyone else. In fact, if not for Father, I would not be in love with her or anyone else! Although others were sent at me when she was here and no one but Father and I were willing for us to be together, no one else will do. I will not desert Father this time, nor will I go out with others, except that we already have an established friendship that is not interested in sex or romance or marriage. I have written many things since I met her! The first was just an impression, I thought, because of how I saw her.

Thanks!

You are welcome to live with freedom to sing, love, and be joyful every day. Too bad that religion is a problem. But it will always be a problem! There are many things to be understood, but they can only be understood as we walk with and agree with Jesus (Jehoshua), the only begotten Son of Jehovah with Mary.

Yesterday was great because Father confirmed that his name, as he revealed it to the Jews by Moses, is the only name that matters. Language is not a problem in dealing with his name. There are many languages, and they are a way of communication for each people. However, no matter the language, the name remains the same by meaning! He is the God of Abraham, Isaac, and Jacob. And he is the Father of the Lord Jesus (Jehoshua)! The only begotten Son was given so that all men, beginning with the Jews and spreading to all others, might be saved and restored to union with Jehovah our father and God. He is the one and only one who can help us have what we all desperately need! I am blessed to be a believer in the truth that Father has and is giving us in Jesus!

Loving a Woman

A man cannot love a woman and bring her head down in shame by the disrespectful sexual use of her body, the Temple of Jehovah, even if she says she wants it that way. And Ellen is very, very, very special! In the midst of tens of thousands, she stands out and above them all. It seems she doesn't know who she is. But because of me, she is troubled by the state of her life.

Three Beautiful Israeli Ladies: Eve, Eva, and Ellen

One day, in November 2015, I went to Dadeland Mall in search of a Breck hairbrush. Instead of finding the brush, I met a most beautiful and angelic-looking young lady, Eve. She introduced me to Deep Sea Cosmetics from the Dead Sea of Israel. I bought products and was rewarded more products for buying. She gave me a facial as proof of quality, and I was greatly impressed but even more by her natural youth and beauty.

One day, in 2016, I went to the mall in hopes that I might see her again. As I walked through the mall, I was approached by a group of young Israeli youths. They offered me samples of the products, and I told them that Eve had sold me two years' supply of them. A lovely, excited young lady asked my name. I told her that I was William, and she exclaimed, "Eve's William?" and ran and gave me a big, warm hug. And thus began a sales love affair that ended with her selling me the rest of the products out at the time, and she left to go to New York to meet her mother and to get an operation. Before she left, she introduced me to a fellow coworker and a new arrival, Noshem. She was our connection until it was evident that Eva would not be returning.

One day, Noshem was working at the Dolphin Mall and invited me to come. There I met a beautiful nineteen-year-old (by appearance) and was told that she was married to the boss. Surprised, I asked her if she was old enough to be married. She said yes and that she was twenty-nine years old. I thought I would never see her again.

However, I was invited to have dinner with a group of her associates at the Cheesecake Factory. It was canceled, but I was dressed and was ready to go out, even if just for a drive.

I was headed in the direction of the mall and then to the beach, when I got another call, inviting me to come for dinner. I arrived, parked, and found the group. We were seated in the restaurant, and she sat next to me as close as the chairs would allow. Her name was Ellen, but I didn't remember it. But I fell in love with her. Though not as pretty as I remembered Eve to be, she was more beautiful. Besides, I had time away from work with her, and she liked me and told the others in Hebrew, and she told me that she told them. Everything about Ellen is beautiful! From head to toe, she is a special creation of God. She told me that she was not married but lived with her boyfriend and that was why they said she was married.

Good things come to those pure in heart and those who would be deceived rather than to deceive.

I thought that the lady between Eva and Noshem was a great and beautiful lady. She was very pretty, but Lady Ellen far exceeded her when it came to myself. And I found out that I love someone that I should love, not to buy from or see on a regular basis. These lovely ladies are exclusively selected to sell the best personal care products I have ever come across and used. However, I have more than I am using daily.

I have more products than I can use on a daily basis. Yesterday, I sought to buy Wave Hand and Body Lotion from Ellen because it is the translation of her real name. She did not have it for sale, and I bought five containers of a premier brand that she recommended.

My wanting to buy them right then was a startling surprise to her. She called Vided to take the order. Vided ended up selling me two other items I was not wanting to buy, but she/they gave me a very great price.

I wanted a picture of them together, but Ellen suggested a selfie, and Vided took it after the transaction was done. I looked her full in her face and eyes and what a natural beauty she is! It seems she has no idea just how beautiful and attractive she is, and that adds to her beauty! Elden, her boyfriend, seems not to know who she is or does not appreciate her. Unless the relationship is stranger than I imagine, one month would be more than enough to make a lifetime formal commitment. Her price, far above all gems of the earth, is far too great to risk losing.

She did mention having children in a couple of years. But she seemed adamant about not being in a marital relationship with him. She appears to be the most desirable woman I have met. She is fluent in several languages also. This fact about her reminded me of Jacquelyn Kennedy!

Thanks be to Jehovah our father and God, and Jesus, his only begotten Son, there is hope for tomorrow and today! As Paul wrote and Travis sings, all things work together for the good of his children and Jesus's siblings. Sometimes things happen that bring pain, sadness, and a sense of solitude. But all work out the necessity of growth in the world in our lives. For if there were no such things, we would not know the power and authority and grace Father has given us and how he delivers us.

Some people, impetuous and void of understanding, incite contempt for themselves while thinking they're intelligent.

Many problems arise between people because of lack of communication of the truth in their relationships.

On November 2015, I went to the Dadeland Mall in search of a Breck hairbrush. I had bought the last one that I owned from there. I walked the mall in search of a store or a kiosk for the brush! I walked into the space of an angel who asked, "Where are you from?"

I replied, "From Mississippi and Miami." Then she began to engage me in her cosmetics from the Dead Sea of Israel. She offered to show me some things about my skin, and the results were astoundingly amazing!

She put a mask on, treated my eyes with serums, and as she treated me, she told me, "I love you!"

That was no problem because I am a person of love, and I responded, "I love you too!" As she treated me, she asked how old I was. I told her and asked how old she was, remembering that in America, men don't ask that of women. She had no problem with it and told me that she is twenty-two years old. I was impressed with her accent and everything else about her! She was simply gorgeous! I could not believe that such a beautiful young woman could be serving me in this capacity and that she was a real, live human being! She was very skilled in both her care of my skin and in getting me to buy her products. I was rewarded several items for buying certain packages. That was two years ago this month! I used two cards to pay for the products, and I never used them out of her sight until I met others from her country! I had looked for her in the mall on other occasions but never saw her again to this date.

She and I communicated by text several times, and I cannot believe that we actually flirted with each other. I knew that it had to be about her selling her skin-care products. She went out west, and while she was there, her boyfriend told me that he was there too, and I encouraged him to keep her. He said that they broke up, and I encouraged him to do whatever he could to restore the relationship. All that time, he was checking out my demeanor to see just what I felt for her. She was twenty-two years old! What could there really be between us? He said that she liked older men. Then he asked how old I was. I said much too old! But a definite connection was made between us. It had nothing to do with romance! Besides, she had the makings of one a lot younger than twenty-two.

By chance that I might see her again, I went to the mall. I was also still looking for my hairbrush because the one I lost, somehow, was very good, and my hair loved its treatment! It made my hair soft, wavy, and easy to handle! As I walked toward the children-and-furniture store of Macy's, I turned the eastward way, and as I walked, I came across the same kiosk! There was no Angel there, as I expected! However, as I walked several of her associates approached me and I told them that I had purchased two years' worth of products from my Angel! One lovely and enthusiastic young woman asked my name! I told her, and she exclaimed, "Angel's William!"

I responded, "Yes!" and she ran to me and gave me the best hug I had received to that date! As I remember, I had not had the touch of such a woman in years! Since I was Angel's customer, and her first, my second Angel invited me to a special treatment! She called her on the phone. Angel and I talked with her, and together they got me to buy other products and used their points to give me a discount and aid me in buying. I gladly received the treatment and bought a small-priced skin-care product! She treated me like someone very special and with TLC (tender, loving care). She asked me to come back to see her again, and I did! And so began a love affair as customer and skin-care specialist! She also told me that she loved me! Somehow it was transmitted that I responded well to being told that I was loved. And it is true to this very date. My Father is love, and I want to be just like him! So is his only begotten Son, Jehoshua, love!

As time went on and as we interacted, we grew fonder of each other, and the highlight of my days was to see her! I can really only say that I grew fond of her! One day, she invited me to a party but never told me when. She had given me an address but no date and time. The next time I met them, I was asked what I did on a certain date. As a customer, she always managed to get me to buy products even when I could not afford to do so. One day I told her that I didn't have any money, and she replied that I had credit and that it was better than money! I tried to explain that the more one uses credit, the less his credit and money! Somehow, she didn't understand that or wouldn't! In our fondness for each other, we inquired whether we were married. I had married a foreigner to help her, and she left town and the state after she was legal. I lost contact with her and thought that we were divorced. After Angel, two showed interest in marrying me, and I became even more fond of her after telling her that at twenty-nine years old, she was too young! She seemed disappointed, and the next day, she brought another associate. As we three sat and talked, without any relation to our conversation, she said, "And you're too young for me!" She was very pretty but too small in stature for my consideration.

But I asked, "How old are you?"

"Thirty-two," she replied.

"And what is old enough for you?" I asked.

"Seventy-two, at the least," she replied.

After I saw that I was the subject of conversation in our absence from each other, I decided that I would apply myself to loving and possibly marrying this beautiful young lady. I went to the courts and requested proof of divorce from the wife I had before marrying the one of foreign descent and her! One was found, and the last was not! I went to the marriage division of the courts, acquired a copy of the license, and went to see how to go about divorcing her. I bought the packet and was advised that it would take at least six months. That devastated me and made things seem impossible. Also, I began to regret not following the instructions Father had given me before she and I were married ten years! If not for that delay and inaction in obeying Father, I could possibly have been married to her! She was awesome and very sexy, and she used well her feminine ways to sell to men! I just liked her, and she did not use that tactic on me, or did she? One day, she was selling to a man, and I saw that she had him in her complete grips! I asked if he were buying, and that gave him some relief, but she called me to the side and told me that she is selling. I sat around the corner in a comfortable chair. When she finished, she came and asked me not to interrupt when she is selling. But sometimes, even with him, my skin was a testimony to what the products could do. And they really do work for me, all over. But I do have to use them.

However, she was not the one for me. Although she had told me not to believe Israelis because they lie, she also told me lies. Nonetheless, I loved her and wanted to be around her. In fact, one day, when I was there and she wanted me to buy something, I explained that I came to the mall because I wanted to see her. She smiled, and then she seemed to say to herself, *I have got him now!* Then she told me that she had made no sales, and she needed me to buy something because my buying brought her success (she used the word *luck*). She had told me that people come to the mall because they have money. I reiterated that I came because I wanted to see her. Yes! She squeezed another buy out of me! Meanwhile, I am only using these products when with them.

She became sick, and I could not see her for a couple of days. When she returned, she informed me that her mother wanted her to meet her in New York to have surgery. I felt lonely for her already. She said that she would leave her possessions here so that she would have to return. I suggested that she invite her mother here. That seemed a good idea to her. But before long, she was gone to Israel. I continued to visit with her thirty-two-year-old associate and another who had just come there to replace her, unknown to me! I latched on to her because she was my only contact with Angel II!

Before she left for New York, her associate, for whom I was too young, told me that someone had taken her footwear, as she had left them outside to air out. I volunteered to buy her replacements, and we bought her shoes and socks. I bought some other things from Macy's and got a free gift card. I gave it to Miss Too Old For Me.

Seeing this, the replacement asked me to buy her a small gift. That was very unusual to me! I always give out of my heart whatever I will. However, she and I kept in touch so that I could know what was going on with Angel II. One day, she was working at the Dolphin Mall, and we talked, and I asked if she wanted me to meet her there. She was too happy for that. She gave me directions, and I went! We had trouble finding each other, and as I looked for her, I met another young lady who had graduated from Florida International University, and I had promised to give her a graduation gift. But she disappeared, and I had no way of contacting her.

A Prayer for Eva

Father Jehovah,

You know Eva far better than I do since you knew her before you formed her in her mother's womb. Thanks for making her such a lovely and warm lady! Though she is young and beautiful, I love her like we are close in age. I don't know why you allowed me to meet her, but I am glad you did. Sometimes, like now, when I cannot reach her to know how she is doing, I miss her and feel really lonely for her. You know what kind of thoughts go through my mind and what the results will be.

I long for her like I long for the end of a long, hard day's work. My heart aches for her and even more so to know what our relationship should be and how soon we can get it on. I long to hold her in my arms and gently squeeze and caress every part of her body and become one with her. Yes, sir, I want to give her pleasure in her body, mind, and spirit, all to your glory.

If I were in your will with my desire, give me your wisdom and strength so that I may know and do with and for her what I should. Father, this has turned out to be a prayer for me to have Eva. Now I pray for her. She left going to NYC for a meeting with her mother and to have surgery. It turns out that she was taken to Israel to get treatment, and I have conflicting information about her. I pray that all she's told me is true and that you are pleased to hear my prayers for her and you are waiting for me so you can heal her and restore her. Even if you don't give her to me, please take care of her and bless her with all that you have for her to the glory of your name, Jehovah, and your begotten Son, Jesus! Amen!

I should have turned to the left to meet my friend when I entered the mall, but I turned to the right, and I heard my name shouted out! *William!* I looked up, and it was she! We ran to each other and hugged, and I lifted her from her feet and twirled her around. Then she took me to the kiosk where I was to meet Ms. Notfar. When we three met, there was tension in the air between the two of them, and the graduate gracefully excused herself and went back to her kiosk.

Ms. Notfar took me for a walk in the mall, brought me to a store, and showed me some purses, one of which she wanted me to buy for her! I looked and followed her around, observing her taste. Snake skin! I didn't care for that. Then another day, my birthday, I went in to buy her a gift. I looked around, and a lovely young lady helped me with the selection and gave me a price that was far below the price that it actually cost! I never looked inside to see the price. It was also outside, and she had removed it. The salesclerk did. I thought I was paying 60 percent off, and I bought a change purse and an ID-and-card purse as well, when I saw the total cost. At the end of the day, I gave her the gifts and went home! A day or two later, we met again, and she wanted to exchange them. I was reluctant, but I went along! Who looks a gift horse in the mouth? Anyway, we made the change, and she got much less products than she had gotten as my present, and I added a couple of more dollars!

We walked out of the store in a mildly heated discussion. She asked, "Don't you like me?"

"I do, but don't you know how I feel about Angel II? Did she tell you to do this?"

She said, "No!" She was shorter than both Angels and more aggressive. Out of the blue, she asked to travel to Melbourne with me.

I felt something strange in my groin and said, "No way!" One day I came from radiation therapy and saw her with an older man who had a much-bigger stomach than mine! I knew that they had spent the night together, somewhere. She was still disheveled! And they were smoking, and she looked tired. I had thought for some time that sex might have been a part of the sales! I prayed not!

Sometime earlier, I had gone to meet my other friend, the graduate, and I waited with her as she closed her kiosk while her associate was away. When I came out, I was met by three angry women. I was accused of buying a gift for my friend in excess of $400. It was not true because I had bought her no gift at all. I also had not bought any products from her. Besides, I could do whatever I wanted with funds Father blessed me with, as long as it was good!

One day I came to the Dolphin Mall and walked to the kiosk of my friend, the graduate. She was there with a lovely lady who looked very young! She was introduced to me as the boss's wife, before that, as the model who graced the kiosk. I looked at her inquiringly, and that was when the graduate added, "She's married to the big boss."

I looked at her in disbelief and asked, "You're old enough to be married?"

She said, "Yes! I'm twenty-nine!" That was unbelievable! But I took her at her word!

Before I met her, the same day that I first came to Dolphin Mall, I met the roommate of Angel II! She said, "I'm the one who called you for Angel II." I gave her a very warm thank-you hug! At the very moment that she called me, I was praying for Angel II and about to forget about her because she did not let me know anything about her condition! She knew how I cared for her!

On a Friday night, the boyfriend of Angel II's roommate invited me to celebrate the Shabbat with them at their home. It was July 1, 2016, I believe. I was in radiation therapy treatments, and my bladder was out of control. So I declined because I didn't feel good going to someone's home and spending so much time in the restroom. I told him so, and he replied, "We're family." I began to regain control of my bladder later in the late afternoon, and I got another call inviting me to meet them at the Cheesecake Factory in the mall. Since I was feeling better and not meeting at someone's home, I agreed. I showered, dressed, and announced that I was going out. Then I got a cancellation call! Well, I was dressed to go out, and I was doing just that. I got in the car and began driving toward the mall, and then I was going for a drive on the beach. As I was driving, I got another call, inquiring my whereabouts. I announced my whereabouts and plan. Then I was told that the meeting was back on. I continued to the mall with directions on the GPS. I parked in the garage and found them. They were sitting outside, waiting to be seated and for others to arrive. They were smoking, and so I greeted them and stood as close to them as I could bear the smoke. She was there! She was dressed in black, with shorts that revealed the most beautiful legs.

We talked outside for a while, and then we were seated at a long table. The boyfriend of Angel II's roommate sat with her along the wall in the booth, and I chose a seat across from them. To my surprise, she pulled up a chair next to me. She was very close, but I didn't lose my composure. She asked about my feelings for Angel II, and I confessed that I cared for her a lot. She asked if I were married, and I said yes. I had just learned a few days before then that I was still married. She said that she was not married and that they introduced her as married because she lived with her boyfriend. I asked if they shared with each other as married people, and she said yes. I said, "You're married then." She emphasized that she was not married. She said that she might get married in a couple of years, then have children. She spoke to her associates in Hebrew and then told me that she told them that she liked me. I replied, "I like you too," and added, "You're awesome!" I felt a little silly afterward, but she was awesome! Angel II was perfect. I told her that with loss of control of my speech. So I meant it from my heart. But now I sit next to a lady who is the epitome of womanhood! The only thing wrong is that she's living with her boyfriend. Is he crazy? She's the kind of woman who, the minute two available people meet, gets married in seconds. Had I been available, I would have! I thought she must not want to.

Dinner was over, and several went outside for a smoke. I sat there with her and a couple of others across the table from us. She excused herself and went to the ladies room. When she came back, she asked me to come with her. I went gladly, and it was like I was floating! I did not know the customs of my new friends, so when our food came and we were eating, she offered me to eat from her plate! I declined because I had much too much to eat. Big mistake. But she did not give up. She asked if I wanted her to save me some of her food? Bigger mistake. I said no. Later, I asked the boyfriend if he wanted to share my food. He said, "No! I'm eating with my girlfriend!" *Wow!* What did I miss? By "she liked me," did she mean that she wanted me for a boyfriend? She's already taken! Nonetheless, they are not married, and she likes me! We're outside now, and her associates are smoking, and therefore, I stand off a bit because of it. They talk, and then she went toward the car. I walked beside the one who paid for my meal. It was in celebration of my upcoming birthday. Let's call her Super Saleslady. As she and I walked to meet

Most Beautiful, Super Saleslady asked where I was parked. I said in the garage. She asked why, and I responded that it was because there was no other parking, and I didn't know where they were parked. Reluctantly, I left them and drove home. I was so excited that I took the long way home and drove slow. I began living for the first time in many years. It was as though I was asleep until she came into my life. I was inspired to write about these three beautiful ladies from Israel that I had met. At that point, I didn't know that I loved her beyond friendship! But my days were complete when I saw her, and my nights were spent in anticipation of when I would see her again.

I believe I spent every day from then walking the mall, observing them all, and praying for their success. I was taking radiation therapy for prostate cancer and walked the mall Monday through Friday after the treatments finished for those days. Finally, in September, the treatments were finished, and I brought the certificate to her to show and tell. An associate was with her, and when I handed her the certificate of completion of radiation therapy, the associate looked at it too. Neither of them said anything, but I could see that they wondered why I showed it to her. If by now they didn't know how much I loved this twenty-nine-year-old, they'd never know. I had walked the mall until she came on duty. Signs of my walking were all over me, except I smelled good. One of the radiation therapists told me that she wished that all of their patients were like me—bladder full (except for one time), clean and smelling good in the treatment area, and easy to handle. So when I showed her my certificate, she told me I could go home now. I needed to because I had to get up early to beat the traffic and find suitable parking and to walk so as to void any food ready to come out! And also, to get any gas out of my system. These are the things the technicians appreciate when treating patients. But I was hardly ready to leave her.

But home I went, and I slept very well after taking a shower, eating, and taking medications for my diabetes. Some people tell me not to claim ailments as my own. But Jesus said that he came for the sick, not the well. And since the sick are well, he can do nothing for them. Therefore, I acknowledge whatever is ailing me, and I take it to him. You know that he works all things for our good, don't you?

Yes! Even sickness and diseases. But he is with me in mine and keeps me going with little adversity because of them.

My love for Most Beautiful began to grow more and more with each passing day. I tried resisting it because she has a boyfriend. But in the Spirit, I am told that he is not her boyfriend and that they don't belong together. I believed this to be true from Father, but I also took her at her word. From time to time, she shows signs of wanting to kiss and be kissed by me. One day, I passed by and gave her something, and when I was leaving, she asked me to wait a while, and then the owner of the kiosk, the boyfriend, came by. They talked and then put on a show of affection that was very awkward for them both. I watched as they did, in bewilderment, because that was not necessary. I had already conceded that they were together, and so they didn't have to do that to me. When they were finished, he left, giving a strange look of displeasure at me! She returned to my side, seeming to want a kiss from me, and I felt like giving her a kiss. Instead, I asked, "Is that why you wanted me to stay?" I turned and walked away, and she watched me as I went. Father told me to turn around and look. She was watching me as I walked away!

I went away, heartbroken and determined that it was over. Father said, "No!"

I asked, "Didn't you see what she did?"

He said, "Don't believe what they show you and tell you. Believe what I tell you." So until this day, I believe what Father tells me about her. In fact, she is the reason that I am here in Israel right now. I had planned and hoped that she would come with me, but she left Florida before all things were completed with me. And I pleaded with her to let me see her before she left. I thought the worst for me without her. At times, I thought I felt life sifting out of me. At a checkup with my primary doctor right after she left, the doctor heard something strange going on with my heart. He ordered an EKG immediately. He heard right. My heart was really broken because she left and would not let me see her before leaving. I did not tell the doctor this. Like her, he might have thought that I was crazy too. I'm seventy-one years old and in love with an actual twenty-two-year-old! I must admit, it really does sound crazy! I would not have chosen this in a million lifetimes. But who am I to tell Father who to make me love like this or not to?

We exchanged texts, she and I, on two Instagram accounts that I have and on Facebook. I told her that I needed her. She asked why. I sent her a copy of my divorce summons that I was sending to my wife. She asked what I wanted her to do, and I told her that I wanted her to marry me. She asked if I knew how crazy that sounded. Also, why did I want her to marry me? I said so that we could be the happiest people we know and please God in all that we are! She said that she was disconnecting from me on the account. That she did! I thought for days that she meant altogether! Later on, I saw that we were still connected on Facebook and on my Note 4 Galaxy smartphone. But I would not contact her for fear that I would lose all contact with her.

When I first began to love her, I asked a group of pastors to pray for me concerning this affair. I was totally out of my league. One pastor told me that it was a trap and that they would kill me. I'm not real sure about the kill part. But he often laughed at me. He had no compassion for me and what I was going through. I don't share easily my personal life for this very reason. And many other people hurt for lack of someone to care for them and listen to their concerns. The world would be a much better place if we all did listen to each other. I took my best friend and her husband to see her. When I asked her if she thought she was beautiful, she said, "No!" And she had great concerns that they would hurt me. Well, that has happened, and I still cannot get her out of my head or heart! But it is not her that hurts me. It is my slowness to have obeyed Father years ago that hurts me. Had I known he had her for me, I would have jumped at getting that divorce. But she was only about ten to twelve years old at that time! A definite minor and cause for prosecution for pedophilia. Of course, I want nothing to do with that.

One day, after I had regained a measure of composure, I went back to the mall to do my prayer walk, wherein I pray for both clients and vendors. I pray that customers have a safe environment there, buy well, and get good to great prices, while the vendors make great sales and make lots of profit. I don't always say this as I walk. Father knows why he has me there! Anyway, while I walked, I met a new girl whom I'd met before my friend, Most Beautiful, left. It was on a Monday that I went in and sat down at Starbucks and was making entries on my phone, when I heard a familiar voice. I looked up, and it was the boyfriend. He kept walking around Starbucks and talking on the phone as he walked. He walked toward the kiosk and disappeared before I finished my entry. After finishing, I went to look for him. I was told that he went to the other kiosk, but I didn't chase him. I left.

On Wednesday of that same week, I was there again, and as I walked, he came from my right and surprised me, and we greeted as friends. How's that for a boyfriend to greet a suitor of one's girlfriend? Clearly, Father was right and proved it! But he had proved it long before then. The week before Father's Day 2017, I drove to Melbourne to look for a home there. On the way, I was impressed with Father assuring me and getting me to my favorite gas station to get gas. I had asked if I could make it, and he said, "Yes!" At times it appeared that I wouldn't. He asked, in my questioning, if I didn't trust Him. I said, "Yes, sir!" And I continued on and had twenty-seven miles left on the range. When I gassed up and continued on my route, he told me not to look there. He further told me to ask her to help me find a house. I thought he had in mind that she would marry me and live there with me!

I did as he told me, and she referred me to her boyfriend. We talked and were ready to do some looking. However, I explained that I was in the process of getting a divorce and not ready to buy, only to find a house that I wanted. He asked why I had asked Most Beautiful to have him look. I told him that Father told me to ask her. Once I had their address, I was prompted by Father to use an address-verifying site to check out his address. There it was! He and another woman bought the house last year as husband and wife. I never told them that I knew or how I knew. But I did tell another former employee, who is still friends with him, that he was married to another woman. She had already, more or less, confirmed the same.

Ellen,

What I feel for you is real in my heart and mind. Though I have tried to shake it off, as you suggested, it is not happening. I am caught between two spheres of influence, what you want in a relationship with me and the will of Jehovah, our God and Father for us. As I reflected on my life forty-three years ago, I find myself in a similar predicament.

There was a beautiful young woman who came to work as an associate in the office in which I worked. The first day we met, something connected us. We were a lot closer in age than you and me. We never held hands, and our lips never touched, but our hearts often beat as one. Roberta Flack recorded a song, "Killing Me Softly with His Song," and one day after I treated her to lunch, we had a disagreement about something. Nobody said anything to us. All of a sudden, she and I began to sing the song. First it was soft, and then it grew louder and more harmonious until a coworker said, "Enough of this strumming and singing." Just like that, with song, we were on one accord again. Later on, she invited me to a play at a school wherein she and her older sister were students. I met them there, and we were seated on the front row at the center. The play was well presented, and an actor came and stood right over us, and he asked a question, looking directly into my eyes, and he looked until I responded. She was unhappy that I did. After the play and stage calls, I wanted to greet that actor who stood over us but she didn't. I went backstage and congratulated him for his performance, and I returned, looking for her, but she was nowhere to be found. I was disappointed and started for home. I had felt that she and I might be a couple for life. But since she was not with me to give congratulations,

29

I thought maybe not. As I drove, I encountered a battle of wits with a spirit. Because of its power, I presumed it was Father's. As I drove down a narrow SW 117th Avenue in February 1973, I tried resisting the spirit's will for me to be with her. I resisted until my vision was black, and I felt great pressure on my head that was taking away my consciousness. I relented, and immediately, my vision returned, and the loss of consciousness was halted. I drove home and went to bed, but the spirit continued to deal with me.

I find myself in a similar kind of love for you, Ellen. Except it was you who initiated our relationship. You were introduced to me as the wife of the boss. I looked at you, so young in appearance, and I asked, "Are you old enough to be married?" And you responded, "Yes, I am twenty-nine." I was done with you, as far as I was concerned. But later, Adriam invited me to dine at his and Vided's home. Because of my lack of continuity, which I was facing due to medical treatment, I declined because I would be embarrassed to frequent the bathroom. But later, things began to get better, and I received a call to meet him and others at the Cheesecake Factory. I agreed, got dressed, and was about to leave when I got a call, calling off the dinner.

I was dressed and had informed my household members that I was going out. So I decided to locate the restaurant anyway then drive to the beach. As I did so, I got a call, saying dinner was back on. I was given the address, and I came. As we were seated, you sat next to me as close as the chairs would allow. I was not displeased. *But why is a beautiful, married woman sitting so close to me?* I thought. Then you began to explain that you live with your boyfriend and have done so for years and want a baby in a couple of years, but you are not married. I asked whether you live as a married couple, doing the things that married people do, and you said yes. I said, "You are married!" But you insisted that you were not married. Because I thought I wanted to marry Eva, I went downtown to get a proof of divorce, only to find out that my wife who deserted me hadn't divorced me and I am still legally married. When you asked me that night, I said yes, but Eva had already informed you all about me.

You spoke with your family and friends, in Hebrew, and then you turned to me and said, "I told them I like you." I am not sure what you mean by that, but my heart began to take a liking to you. My eyes love having you in view. I loved seeing you, and I still do. Not seeing you for so long and not knowing if I ever will again has prompted me to write this, reflecting on the past forty-three years. I am wondering if I am crazy, delusional, or if Jehovah our father and God, really wants us together and whether all that I have seen with you as my wife is true and forthcoming or not. I am even thinking of checking into a mental health institution to be checked out. One thing I am sure of, if they are not allied with Jesus and Jehovah, I am in big trouble! But they are more than capable of getting me out, Jehovah and Jesus. But I have this question for you. Do you love and want me or not?

As for me, there is no question! I love and want you for the rest of my life, however long or short it may be. You have encouraged me to love Israel, his people and language, and most importantly, Jehovah our God and Father, with knowledge, more than I ever have. I see his only begotten Son in you.

I am not the average man. You are definitely sexy and alluring, even without the clothing you wear sometimes. I have told you before that I love you more than your sexiness. But if you marry me, you would not be disappointed in that area or any other because Father has shown me undreamed-of blessings, and who would imagine that we could experience such today?

A few weeks ago, you questioned if I knew that you were playing when you said you were twenty-nine years old. Without Father's blessings, anyone over fifteen years my junior is too young for me. But I have recently learned that when we are one with Father and are of adult age, there is no "too young" or "too old." Only Father's will be done, and we who do it are willing to please him. I am. When it comes to life, I am not playing. Yes, I laugh and enjoy life events, but I take them as seriously as required.

Hello, Father! I know that you saw what she did and you know and understand why. You are more than wonderful for having me to love her still. We are more than she, the earth filled with people, and you still love us with the purest heart ever. You are God, and you see and know the whys and understand every thought of every person. Were it not for you, I would not continue to love her and pray for you to bless her with success and a great life.

But I am more than pleased to do your good will. I am assured that you always do what is good. And no matter what happens, when we, and more specifically, when I, obey you, we already have the victory. I know that you know why she acted the way she did, but does she know? Will you protect her when she shows herself to be the opposite of what you tell her about herself by my mouth? I pray you will and give her to a son suitable for her from among your obedient and holy sons. It is more than obvious that I am not pleasing to her, even if I were the only man on earth. I still find her attractive because of the way you've made her. And I still love her and like to see her because of what you have placed in me for her. Like Jesus asked, can you remove this cup from me? Nonetheless, your will be done in my and with my life. It is already yours. I don't know why this one is so important to you, and I don't understand why you placed such love in my heart for her. You have many more who are willing to give themselves to me.

I only live to please you, and I will love you and wait for you in all things. I thank you for your plans for me beyond her. And I look forward to the fruition of them. Thanks, Father, for this heart, and thank you for this brown body and all that comes with it. You have done marvelously. This is the only way to live for me.

In Messiah Jehoshua, I love you, Father! Amen!

Father,

I don't understand why I am back to this longing and immobility. She sent me a video of her dancing at a Miami club, her watching TV in bed with a black dog and a white dog in bed with her and zooming in the captions in Hebrew, and finally her taking a selfie. She appears to be alone at 9:16 PM. But that could have been temporary. I am completely confused. We know that, naturally, I should not feel like this for her. And she shows signs of contempt for me and exasperation. I wrote to her boyfriend and tried to explain that my love for her comes from you and is pure. And that I love him too and would like to be his friend and brother. He has not returned an answer. But she sends these photos as messages. Her friend and associates sent videos of her and boyfriend dancing and taking pictures with them, and then they were gone. Only a picture of pizzas was left on her post.

What do I do if I see her? Do I pass by like I don't know her or what? I am listening to hear from you soon, and I will sleep while I wait for you to answer. Thank you, Father. I love and adore you and respect your plans for me. And I don't mind dying for you or being put in jail or even exiled. Your will, at all costs, is my will. Besides yours, I have no will. I just want to know if it is you who guides me and I am not being hustled or slandering your name.

Greselle,

I am writing to you in my profile because I am considering your current state of mourning the death of a very close friend.

I write to tell you that I love you for more than a customer or a friend. Though I feel it proper for us to grow as friends. But somehow my heart has flown to you, and I love you deep down within it. I feel your love for me, but I feel it is not the same as my love for you.

On a scale of one to ten, ten being the highest possible number, you are a ten, and you could have any man you want from any age group. Because you have a life before we met and are busy in it, you don't have any time to devote to me, except when you are at work. I cannot get to know you that way, and I feel our relationship is one way. And that is from me to you. I don't know if I will share this with you or not. I just have to write it down for my clarity of mind.

When you put your makeup on in front of the mirror, you can see a beautiful woman, but what you do not see is the love that you draw or pull from a man like me.

Though you are the total package of a desirable woman in body, I want you for the person you may not have discovered that you are. Without spending personal time alone with you, I cannot know what you know about yourself, nor can I learn what I want and need to know about you.

By the way, your mother and sister are beautiful, but you are the most beautiful to me. I want to know just how beautiful you are deep within your being.

You said you are jealous. I am too, but I can't afford to have jealousy rule my life. I did that once, and jealousy almost consumed me.

We have different but complimentary ways of life when it comes to serving the only living God. I was brought up loving him in Jesus (Joshua) and in different rituals and festivals. As I read the Holy Scripture, I always wondered why I didn't observe the same time and days as you and somehow felt incomplete. So I want to serve Jehovah, our Father and God, as Jesus did. I am not wanting to denounce anything that Jesus opened to us and taught us. Instead, I want to fully embrace everything Father would have us to embrace. When that is done, I may have understood my love for you better and our relationship.

I would love to be the one who has the privilege of seeing you, morning and night, for the rest of my life, now and eternally.

Now I know that I will not share this with you, Greselle. The reason is a greater draw and pull of love from me by a young woman who I believe has no match on Earth today. She is a little younger than you but has an effect on me that I thought you had killed. But just one look into her eyes, and the sound of her voice shook everything I had for any other woman. And I can't have her…I think. She inspires me to write, to feel good, to be young and free, and to write a prose I shared with you earlier. I suppose one reason I am so taken with her is time off the clock. I first saw and met her on the clock and never thought anything of it.

But one evening, we shared a meal, and she recommended salmon, and I recommended eggplant parmesan for her because she doesn't like fish. She offered me to eat with her from her plate. When I declined, she offered to save her dish for me. I also declined that, to my hurt. Others, coupled off, ate that way, and when I offered others to share mine, one fellow said he was eating from his girlfriend's. She and I were too new for that, I thought. But I would like to have her as such and more! Eve was very pretty, as I remember, but she is plain next to Ellen.

Today I saw her, and we had fun around a purchase I made from another vendor. As we parted, our hands held on and lasted to the tips of our fingers. My heart raced, as one about to have a heart attack, I suppose. I sat there for a while to collect my heart, and she was gone. I left the mall, singing and dancing inside and so full of joy!

You could do that to me too, but my heart sinks as I write this. So I suppose she is the only one who has the power to make me feel like this now. Oh, how I love her and Jesus! She looks to me to be his twin sister. But since he was and is without sin, and apparently, she is a sinner by living as married with a man jealous of her being with other men, including myself, in an unofficial commitment. He could marry her today, I believe. She says she loves him, of course, after I asked.

I cannot think of sexual intercourse with her because I see her so *pure!* But given the right relationship with her, I would kiss her all over her body and ask to please her in every way I could. Just who is the woman? Her name translates to "wave," originally. And what a wave of love floods my soul when I see or think of her.

Ellen,

Being in the world and knowing you are here makes my life rich. And sharing time and space in closeness, like the photos we took, makes me so overjoyed that I question my reality. Is it real, what I see, touch, and feel? Is my heart able to keep pace once you have come so close? Jehovah has many beautiful daughters, but you are the most beautiful to me. I have tried to erase you from my heart because you have a special man, but our unspeakable language says that I am yours and you are mine. I would never deny that you are, with Father and Jesus, who matters to me. I tried with another beautiful daughter of Father's, but even she could not come to me even though we love each other. She could not erase you from one corner of my being. Therefore, I await yours and Father's will and timing.

When we played on Friday, my whole body was filled with unspeakable joy, and I could not move before I recollected my breath. I long for this joy eternally. I have loved very deeply before but never like I love you. It is like I cannot move unless it is to you.

You Are My Beloved and Not Another

Many are the beautiful daughters of Jehovah and of men, but you are the only one for me. Yes, I do love, care for, and respect every one of them. But there is only one you and one me. Though you too love, care for, and respect another before you, I am not Jacob or Israel that I should have the elder and then the younger. If I could, she, the older, would hate me because I am totally given to you, and I did not do it, nor do I resist it. I tried and I tried not to love you like this, but my heart only multiplies its affection and love for you. You do not answer my calls or texts, but that does not stop my heart. You tell me that I am big, and I am. But I have been bought at a high price and am commanded by the owner of my soul. If he were not so kind and strong, I would wrench my heart from him even at the cost of losing my life! But he gives me joy and hope throughout each day. Yes, even when I cannot talk to you or see you. Day and night, you and he are my concerns. I want to please him in everything that I am or do. I have become obsessed in an unusual way, and I don't know where I am going or if I am sane. In my natural sane mind, I would love you, but I would not long after you like I do. I was cold when I last saw you as I left your presence. I did not know that you were still on-site. I may have done as you and gone outside to warm up as I studied. I was surprised to see you there. So lovely yet somehow sad. I hope I was not or am not the source of that sadness. If I am, say the word and whatever I need to do to reverse it. I am willing. For your sadness is mine, and your joy is my delight. I have something very important to clear up before I can take you to me, but I am completely yours already. No one else will ever be who you are to me. You are the joy

Jehovah our father and God, blessed me with. But for now, I stand in uncertainty because I did not heed Father's voice some years ago. I have heard everything you have said to me, and I take it all to heart. I love you, and your happiness and joy are my concerns even if I am not the one you choose to fulfill it for you. Father can make my heart happy and glad even if you choose another. But I love you. I love you, and I love you forever!

William, October 21, 2016

Here we are! She didn't want me, and I didn't want her to have me. But here we are! She doesn't want my heart and love, but she's got it. I am caught between two spheres. I love her, and I want to love her with all my heart. I don't know if she should have it, but without asking me, she has complete control. I try to resist, but all I can do is think of her.

When I see her, my heart is torn! I am like glass. Translucent. Everyone who sees me knows that I belong to her, and not one of them is happy about it, if faces tell the truth, that is. Maybe it's because I don't know how to deal with the situation. I have never competed for the love and affection of a lady. Either she was free and for me, or she was for and with another, and I would be a friend. Until now I never thought of infringing upon the established relationship. But here I am, totally and head over heels in love with another man's sweetheart and lover. I don't understand it. I have looked at a thousand beautiful and fine ladies, and not one of them compares to her! In her presence, I try to be cool, calm, and collected. But she looks at me with those eyes of hers, and I lose control. My heart is beating like a racehorse just finishing the big race. Here we are. She and I, face-to-face, and she knows that she has all power over me. She is gentle and kind and speaks to someone on the phone. Yet she keeps her eyes on me. She wants me to say bye before I leave for she must return to work. I finished half of my sandwich and drank my green tea until finished. She is still on the phone, evidently talking to a coworker at another kiosk because when I was going to say bye and visit the other kiosk, she said she had to go there too. Awkwardly, I walked beside her, at her back, and apart from her. I don't know where I stand with her, and the looks people give me, I don't want her to get. After all, I love her supremely and purely.

She's a beautiful woman, with everything in place, yet she is not like other women to me. But here we were!

We arrived at the other kiosk on opposite sides. She greeted a consultant and a customer who were having problems with the transactions. I greeted the other, whom I met there weeks ago, and we chatted. She called me my beloved's friend. Now I know that everyone knows that I belong to her. You see, people today don't say boyfriend and sweetheart. They mostly just say friend. She and I talked about my age and hers. She said that she is nineteen years old but looks twenty-four. I said she could be eighteen years old by her looks. Then she asked how old I was. I asked, "How old do you think?"

She said, "I think fifty to fifty-five, maybe fifty-eight." Then she asked me again. I told her seventy, and she said that I didn't look that old. But here I am, in uncontrollable love with a lovelier lady only two years older than she! I have no idea what she is thinking of, but I can imagine..."dirty old man!"

Well, I am very happy to love her and to be in love with her. But I have no dirty thoughts about her. Not even when I try, I cannot hold that thought for more than a second.

Since she doesn't want me, and as a result, I don't want her, it has to be something much bigger than the two of us. When one looks at her, it is no wonder that I would want her. Any man, with good sense and good vision, would want her for sight alone. But she has a lot more than her good looks going on.

I have been shown some really great things about her by the spirits, and I think that it is the Greatest Spirit, Jehovah, God Almighty! So you see, I am afraid to run to her and especially from her! For me to do so is to run from his will, which I am gladly and cheerfully to do! For everything about me is for him and him alone. He sent many into the world for its salvation, but only one was worthy of that. He begot a son and, though I have sinned, I want to be just like that son. He is known from the Greek, in English, as Jesus and from the Hebrew, in English, as Joshua. This is the short form. The original is Jehoshua. It means Jehovah's salvation. Oh, how I love those names and, of course, hers. I am not ashamed of her, her name, or my love for her though I could easily be, by age, her grandparent. I do love Jehovah, our God and Father, and Jesus with all my being, and I love her!

At my waking, Father impressed upon me trust. Time after time, he has told me that my beloved loves me. I have had trouble believing and wanting to believe it because of her first conversation with me. However, her body language said she liked being near and close to me. But I listened to her with my ears and interpreted what she told me from her mouth, such as "I am not married. I live with my boyfriend, but we are not married."

I asked if they were involved as a married couple, and she said, "Yes."

I said, "Then you are married!"

"I'm not married," she said emphatically.

"Do you love him?" I asked.

"Of course," she replied. But she still insisted that they were not married.

She and her coworkers spoke in Hebrew, and afterward, she told me that she had told them that she liked me. My head was spinning from the awe of her, and I don't remember if I told her that I liked her or not, but I remember telling her, "You are awesome!" And there was and is no doubt about that.

She has shown me, in many ways, that she does love me. I just have not been able to get over her living with her boyfriend as a married couple. I was married. I know how married people are together.

I have also been getting from the spirit that she and the one I think is the boyfriend is a brother. I don't know how that can be because of the pictures she had posted for me on Instagram. Yet Father Jehovah asked me if I trusted him concerning her like I trusted him concerning Hurricane Matthew.

Of course, I must say yes and know that I cannot fool him! Right now, I am feeling like I need to go to her and apologize for being so inept. First, I apologize to you, Father Jehovah. You have never done anything but good for me. And yet because she is even younger than I thought, I doubted both her love and your love for me by giving her to me. So again, Father, I apologize. And I will be speedier and more diligent in handling the business of unencumbering myself of dead weight! I will start with her, if you please, and continue with the other!

Thank you, Father! You are *awesome!* You birth your own begotten Son into a world of religious and sinful men, of whom I am a chief. You crucified him to atone for our sin, cleansed, and gave us your righteousness by and with him, and you give an old thick-headed man like me the love of a beautiful young lady. How can I say thanks, Father? Strengthen me, Father so that my mind is clear, body and energy strong so that I can take care of all that is needed to glorify you and your beloved son Jehoshua!

My Heart Is a Song

Since I met you, I sing all day long.

I was born in a song, and my heart is a continuous song.

Every beat has a melody of its own. And since I met you, Ellen, the airwaves speak only of you.

I listened to hear other names for, surely, you can't be the only one. But when I hear others, my ears are jammed, and my heart starts skipping.

Then your face appears. Your name is in the waves, and my song is restored. Ellen, Ellen, *Elleeeeeen!*

You are my heart, and my heart is my song. My only reason to live is to my heart's song, and you are my heart.

The air is full of singing, beautiful, melodic singing. Every note is your face, every bar is your name, every clef is you. You are my heart. My heart is a song. A beautiful and unending song till I am no more. But I am forever more.

Though I have not seen or heard from my heart, I feel great. I feel confident that my heart is mine forever and that my song will never end.

I was not ready to come home even though I had reason to. But when I opened Instagram, your face appeared. I heard your voice. My heart started racing, and I could not pack fast enough. I was packed now, and the car was loaded. I was off to the station for gas so that I could get back to see you. Traffic was moving fine, and I was going to see my song. Two hours of driving, and bladder needed relief. So I found a place then went back to the race to see my heart. Then all of a sudden, just past West Palm Beach, the traffic started jamming. We came to a stop, then a crawl, then to twenty-to miles per hour and back to stop, crawl, then daylight. Sixty-five miles per hour and grace! I was so excited. I was on my way to see my heart and song. Oh no! Not the stop, crawl again! I programmed GPS for another route, and oh no! I paid to zoom, but instead, more of the same stop and crawl business.

So I wiggled my way in and out and through traffic. I made it! Bladder wanted relief again. Done! I washed my hands and went off to see my song! I looked, and there was no sign. Where could my heart be? I was told that she was gone.

Okay. I went to greet my brothers and her best friend, Sadie, and Sharon were there, preparing to leave as Shabbat approached. I had three oranges for her but gave them to my brothers. I was on the road again, and traffic was worse. A voice said, "She is not gone." There is a reason for my heart and Song not being there when I arrived. I would rest better at home. But I was blocked. I went east, and lanes were backed up. I made a U-turn and headed back west.

I hope that everybody knows what it is to love. When God and those who recognize that their lives depend on him in every way say "I love you," it means just that. There is and are no hidden agenda in those words from God's point of view and of those in him. I do claim to be in him. Have I not shown my love to be without hidden agenda? How many times have I asked for anything but love as I give it? I know that, without a doubt, my life depends on my loving you and not on my getting anything out of you but love.

And guess what? Your life depends on the exact same thing. There can never be peace unless we love each other as God Jehovah loves us. He has open communication with us. That is the only way we can know what he wants of us. We need to do the very same thing with each other. We should forgive each other our misunderstandings and hear each other out so that we respond appropriately.

Appropriately is with care for each other's well-being right now and forever.

If I lose you because I am too stubborn to listen to you, I also lose myself. We are meant to be together and not apart. I met a few people with whom I cannot get a word in edgewise. So I listen, and if we agree, I am satisfied. I don't always have to speak. Besides, I am a better reader of what I have written, which is evidence in every court of what I said and also what you said. But Father has record keepers, and in his court, no lie will tarry.

So I love you. Each and every one of you, I love you. But some, I love you with a different intensity. Nonetheless, it is the same love proceeding from our God and Father Jehovah. And its intent is good and not evil. So talk to Jesus, Jehovah, me, those you agree with, those you disagree with, those you say you love, and those hard to love for whatever reason and especially if you've had some kind of relationship, be it professional, platonic, strong romantic, or whatever. Time is running out, and we never know if we will have another chance to speak. A neighbor was cutting his grass one week or in the same week, and without notice, he is gone. Good thing I started to speak to him after I thought he mistreated an elderly woman. So one big group hug all around the world! Yes, just like on TV, with the recording artists and everybody else. But this time, let's not stop loving each other. Kill that which is for moneymaking only and is destroying the moral fiber of our worldwide society!

Talking to myself: I don't know why you can't get her out of your mind. Her beauty is not of this world. I would love her too. But she is so young. Yes, she is an adult and unmarried, but she's in a relationship that is confirmed by her and her acting. However, you say spirits tell you it's not true. That what you are shown and told are not true. I believe that what you are told by the spirit is true. But only the course of time will prove. In the meantime, do what he tells you, and stop moping and being depressed. Those never got anyone anything but saddened loneliness.

Talking to myself again: I know why you can't get her out of your mind. First, you didn't put her there. Second, she is very lovely, and she is never the same although she is always the same. Third, Father Jehovah has something for you two to accomplish, and lastly, there's so much that one cannot tell. It is living.

I love you more!

It has been days since I have seen you. I know that you know that because you have not seen me in the same number of days. I have seen and visited with others that I have not seen in more days than the days between us seeing each other. I expected to see one, and we had a great time visiting. The other was a great surprise and a confirmation of Father's word to me. Also, a revelation why he chose you for me over her. I am satisfied if I don't see her again because he proved to me that he is doing for her what he promised.

I see you for the first time each time I see you. I never want to leave your presence, but I don't want to overstay my welcome. I don't want to under-stay either. But I rather have you wish I had stayed than that I had left. I did that once. Remember? I wish never to leave your presence. All you have to do is tell me. You already know that

I am yours for the taking. Just one thing to be resolved. Father told me to do it long ago. I resisted because I did that two times before. Had I known he was preparing me for you, I would have done it already. Now that he has brought you to me, I still move too slowly. Sometimes it is because I feel you don't want me. But obedience to Father is more important than my feelings.

With those days, missing you and seeing you tonight makes me love you more. I came out tonight just to see you. When I didn't see you there at the kiosk, I bought your cake pop for the three who were there, and Amore pointed me to you. You look so good and beautiful. No, not at all like you need to lose weight. I only left because I saw you. Know that you have someone you shouldn't leave for any reason, but you are not meant to be. I want and need you with all my heart but only when you want me the same. I am not ashamed of loving and wanting you because I know that it is of Jehovah our father and God. I apologize for not being ready when he brought us to meet. But I beg your patience and indulgence while I obey Father and accomplish this task. I feel that, since I met you, I have no one else to live for, except Father, of course, and then what we're here to accomplish.

When I see you, it is enough for a while. Then I can stay away from the malls until I must see you.

But I would enjoy a more relaxed atmosphere with you.

My! How strange the turn of events and relationships on Earth are. I now know why things are not as Father would have them on Earth. Though some vehemently deny that humans have a choice before they know Father and walk with him, it is not the truth. Even as I write this, I am facing situations that have resulted from my bad choices and slowness to obey Father. I don't know where I would be, but I do know that I would be in a more favorable situation had I been quick to obey him. That's so because Father always guides his faithful and obedient ones in the ways of righteousness and prosperity, to the glory of his name, Jehovah. He led Jehoshua (Jesus), and he walked in favor all the days of his life. Only in the days of the betrayal and horrible mistreatment and crucifixion did he seem to be forsaken. But his rewards for steadfast obedience are power to take up everlasting life in the crucified and glorified body, all of Father's power in heaven and on Earth, and power to share all the benefits with those who believe and receive him. And they (we), with him, share in all that he has. Yes, we're joint heirs (siblings) with him!

We, though very sinful and unclean, are made as pure and holy as he and Father Jehovah. None of our past is held against us here or in eternity. And we hold nothing against any because this is the sign that we are not with Father and him!

I communicated with you on Instagram and Facebook messenger on the eve of the Shabbat, and things didn't go well between us. I declared my love and full intent of my heart to you. You said that you couldn't comply with my desire for us and said that you were cutting our conversation. And indeed, you did, on my international phone number on Instagram. You wiped out all the conversation we had there and completely wiped out any access to your profile.

At first, it did not matter because you had no compassion for me. And you said that you were leaving. I begged to see you before you left, but you would not.

I saw that you allowed me to continue following you as a friend on Facebook, but I dared not chat you there. I love you, and you know that very well. I know that you are loving me too. I also know that our love is approved by the highest god, our father. Why he picked the two of us is beyond my comprehension, but I am bound to his will. I didn't know what my purpose here was, but he is teaching me, and you are a part of the lesson and, seemingly, the purpose as well.

I can't sleep right now because I also found that you are still allowing me to follow you on Instagram, and I couldn't resist watching your story. You are the only person I care to see or be with. You and Toto are such a beautiful sight to see. I am lost without you. I keep going because I believe that I have success in Father's will ahead. Yet I feel my will to live without you ebbing away, and I must finish my purpose without you so that I can go home in peace and with honor. I am here for you anytime you want to do Father's will with me. I am certain that no one, save those who have already accomplished Father's will, will be happier or richer than we. Father Jehovah has told me that the richest people are those who have his full support. He said it originally another way. "The richest person in the world is the one who can ask me for anything for himself or a loved one, and my answer is, you've got it!" The riches Father gives is eternal, as well as temporal. I love you, Ellen alone, and I hope to love you eternally. It is now 1:16 AM. Hopefully, you are sleeping peacefully and dreaming, and I will be doing the same soon. I love you, and I cannot and do not want to stop.

My heart is broken because you left me with a story on Instagram with Toto. I am saddened that my eyes didn't have the opportunity to look upon your form before you left, nor was I able to feel your gentle touch. I visited my doctor today, and he actually detected my heartbreak. He heard irregular beats and ordered an EKG, which confirmed what he heard. I didn't tell him that you had left me heartbroken.

Since you have done this, I don't know how much longer I am going to be here. I am at a loss of how to go forward. But forward I go, and I hope not to live with this heartbreak very long. I got a call from my wife. The constable has served her the summons for the divorce. There is nothing for her to sign except for the receipt of the summons. Now I can renew my passport and finish booking my visit to Israel. I wouldn't mind leaving the Earth from there. I want to see several things of interest and maybe see Leel. We've communicated, and he wants to see me when I am there.

If I were to see you when I am there, my life would be complete, and I could leave the Earth, Father-willing. I certainly don't want our time together to be short, but *que sera, sera!* How I have lived till now is a real puzzle since you *came!* And your leaving has left a big void. I won't tell you that I love you anymore. It seems a mute statement now though very true. I go on.

The Joy of Loving You

Many years ago, I began to ponder and to search to know love and its meaning and how to apply love in life. Until I met you, I really did not have a clue. Oh yes. There is the Holy Scripture passage about love, written by Saul of Tarsus, who was later named Paul. It is a really beautiful passage, and it holds love in the very highest esteem. Love is God. Someone objects, saying that God is love, but love cannot be God. By man's logic, when it is logic, it must be that if God is love, then love is God. The confusion comes when we try to impose on love what we call love. Now that I have met you, I am assured that, for the very first time, I know love. And I know love intimately even though we have only hugged as a sign of our love for each other.

God, Jehovah, created humans, people, in his image. "Let us make people in our image and in our likeness," he said. And that is exactly what they did. They? The eternal godhead of which all are holy and active participants in the creation and especially in the making of people (Adam), God (Gen. 1:26–28).

Jehovah is love, and therefore, he created people to be love also. Since I met you, I understand that better than at any time before. And though I love all others, you are the only one that owns everything about me. Others want me, and they have me but not like you! You are the only one Jehovah approves for me. There is nothing that I can withhold from you that is good.

Father's favor rests upon me, and I can bless others but not like I can bless you. Whether we are near or far, my heart is filled with joy because I know that you are and that we have a connection that is made by our father, and no one can separate us because no one can separate us from him! So I will bless Jehovah in Messiah Jehoshua at all times. His praises are continually in my mouth.

And because of you, my heart is a continual song, and my song is you. At first, I was concerned about loving you like I do. But quickly, Father taught me what I share here. You belong to him and are in him and, therefore, love (noun). No! Father is not a verb, but he makes all actions possible! Now do you see how loving you is so joyous? I sing you all day long. I see you all day long. I think of you all day long. And in everything I do, I do with you in mind. Everything that I possess belongs to you. Yes! If my heart and soul belong to you, then so does everything else. And I do it all for you. Yes! But what about Jehovah, you ask? That is very simple. He made you and me in his image and likeness and, therefore, when we love each other with all of our being, we are loving him with all of our being. That is why he says what he has joined together, let no man separate. So miles cannot separate you and me. Oceans and countries far away cannot separate you and me. Why would he join you to me and me to you? I can only think of his love for us and his purpose. He shows me your holiness, and I know that I am holy.

Sometimes you do things that seem to prove me and him wrong. But you and I are the clay, and he is the potter. I most definitely will not tell him not to make me like he has. The joy of loving you is the same as the joy of loving him! When we all find this joy, then he will do what he has purposed. By all, I mean and he means all who are willing and will be willing to be his Holy Temples, and thereby, be saved. He will separate eternally the holy from the unholy. After that, there are no possible changes. I would never want to stop loving you. You bring joy to my loving you. Some people don't understand this. But this moment has been planned from eternity, and my soul is overjoyed. You are my heart, and my heart is my song. I sing you all day long because of the joy I get loving you.

From the heart of my Father to my heart to yours,
William D. Weathers

I have not the slightest idea where you and I will end up. I only know that I love you and want you around me. I have feelings for you that go far beyond the ordinary. Yesterday, I showed a couple of young ladies a video of a deceased singer who looks like me sometimes. Then I began listening to his songs, and each one of them expressed my exact feelings and love for you. And all night long and day, you are filling my mind, thoughts and prayers. I went to the store for a friend. While there, I decided to take a look at Instagram. There you were with a new story. When I viewed it, I saw your pet, Toto, and your sister. I don't know why she's in your story, but no woman but you interest me. No matter how pretty and lovely they are, they are not comparable to you for me. I have told you that I will die, I hope, with you as the last woman I love like this. Actually, you are the only one I love like this. I have loved others but not one of them like this. You make all other women invisible to me except that they are. I search their form and faces to see you. When it's not you, I wonder, as I have asked you, who are you that you should so impress me and have such a hold on me? You're more than young enough to dissuade my affections for you. Why you would have me looking at your younger sister is beyond my comprehension, but I am persuaded that the end of the viewing of your stories is here.

I love you desperately, but I am, by no means, desperate for you. I only want to do my Father's will. How you fit in my life is between you and him.

I am here and thinking about you as usual and always. It is my pleasure to know you and have you on my heart, day and night. I love everybody, every lady, that I met before you. However, it seems you're the only one for me. It does not matter that we have physical years between us. All that matters is that you make me want to live with you the rest of my life. Though we're physically far apart and I can't seem to get a good conversation with you, you seem so close. I am comforted by dreams and daydreaming of holding you in my arms and holding hands and looking into one another's eyes. Your eyes are so beautiful and expressive. I feel your love for me flowing from them and showering me. I adore you so much. All my love and all of me is for you alone. I love you.

I Would Tell You

I would tell you what you mean to me. I would tell you that with all my being. I love you. I would tell you that, since you are gone, I feel lifeless! I would tell you that I love you with love far beyond my capacity and that I want you forever. But I feel that if I tell you all this, you would not care or want to hear that from me. So I write it to myself and keep it in my heart. As long as I live and breathe on Earth, this is my fate with you. I am more than happy to love you. It is my Father loving through my heart and soul. I love loving you.

Ellen,

It has been fourteen days since I last saw you or heard your voice. The silence is deafening! I have all kinds of thoughts going through my mind. I don't know where I am with you. You seem to care about how I feel for you, but you only give minor signs of your care to me.

Others try to push me to another. I do love and care for her. I love the way she hugs me and lays her head on my chest, listening to it beat for you. And as she does so, I hope you will, once and for always, hug me that way and rest your head on my chest and know that it beats only for you.

I long to see you, talk with you, and hold your hands. I want to pour out my words from my heart to you and know that you care and feel the same for me.

I only have memories of the day we met. We sat beside each other at dinner, shared a Sabbath meal, the few times we talked as you worked, and finally, seeing you on the phone with someone, and you said, "Shalom or goodbye, William!"

I wished I were smarter in the affairs between man and woman of the godly kind. I believe I would be happy in your company rather than writing to you what you will not see. If my thoughts are right, I pray the best for you. There is no one else whose happiness means more to me. No, not even mine. If you were happy to be with me, then it would delight me to keep you happy.

I delight to know how to please you. So you only have to tell me what you want. And if it is in my power and it will not displease Father Jehovah, then I will do it with all joy. Though I dread it, I am hoping that young man will not keep you in unrighteousness, but sanctify your bed according to Father's will for a man and a woman.

Ellen,

I love you far more than I know how to deal with. Day and night, you fill my heart and thoughts. I try to get away from being close to where I know you frequent, but find myself being driven to go there. Tonight, I visited the home of two friends so that I might have something and someone else to think about so my heart would not ache so much for you. The first friend was returning from a trip later tonight, and so I visited him and his wife and grandsons for a while. Then I visited my blood brother who was outside and going out. We chatted briefly and then I headed home. I had to travel by your place of business and couldn't help but stop by. It was good because I needed to stop and may not have made it home without that stop.

I have tried to erase you from the place in my heart and mind, which you hold, but I can't! She's a pretty and older woman whom I tried to erase you with. But somehow, even Father won't help me not to love you like I do. In fact, I hear whispers in my head that you love me as I love you. How could that be when I am old enough to be your father or grandfather? I love you without regard to your age being so much younger than mine. As I know, you're the only woman who could keep my eyes and heart from all others even though I must still be nice to them. I told you before I am crazy about you, and without you, I am finding it hard to want to live. Please put me out of misery, and tell me you love me too or that I should leave you alone. If the latter, I will find a way to get you out of my heart and soul. I know it won't be easy.

Seventy Years Old and in Love like a Sixteen-Year-Old

My heart has flown to a beautiful young lady. I don't know how it is. I only know that it is.

I see her face day and night, at all times. She is so lovely. I have talked to God about her, and I hear that she loves me the same as I love her. Except that he is God, I don't know how or why I would be so favored by him. I have the affection of other women, young and old, but my heart belongs to her and my being too. Breathing is not the same since I have not seen her in a few days. It seems like months. I am glad to love her. She is a daughter of the highest god, and he favors me with a heart of love for her, like his.

Jehovah my father makes me love him more by having this young lady as an object of love. She is beautiful and good, like him! I find truth, love, power, and authority to the highest degree. I wonder if I project these qualities on her or if these are revealed by Father.

Dearest Ellen,

It did my heart and soul good to hear "my love" from your lips. I am very happy to love you like I do. I intended to love you like I love all other women and people in the world, but something strange and wonderful has happened. You are the center of my thoughts and vision. I think amorous lyrics of you, and I see visions of you throughout the day and night. My heart beats differently since you came, and my knees don't want me to leave your presence. They speak for my whole body and consciousness. How did you get that kind of power over me? I think and feel that it is from our God and Father Jehovah. Do you think the same?

I know, since I am connected to Father through Jesus, that I have a powerful love, but I didn't know it could be so powerful toward one single young woman, you! You know how I feel about Eva. I care for her immensely, but the way I feel for you supersedes the way I feel for her and every other woman. And if I could say it a billion times, I love you, I would still be short of saying it enough. I love you.

I thank you, Father, that I have this maturity, boldness, and especially the love that flows from you in me. Thanks for loving through me and helping me to understand your love and heartaches for us, as you love a young woman through me. I really do love her and now understand that you really do love us and at whatever the cost. Not only did you crucify your only begotten Son for us, but you made yourself so vulnerable to be hurt to the very core of your being. Now, Father, I love and appreciate you even more. Yes, you are God and very big, but you are a person, just like we are for you made us in your image and likeness.

Father, make me more like your son Jesus and like you. To your glory, give me the wisdom and understanding of how to listen and respond receptively to everyone who needs my best attention. Forgive me for being so inept at responding appropriately and timely to Ellen. Father, bless especially and keep her forever in the center of your heart, so she is holy and pure and washed from all sin. And bless her and me with the relationship you want for us.

Thank you, Father, for setting me free from the burden of loving Ellen. As I know her, she's a wonderful person, with some discrepancies, like knowing and telling her age and devotion to you. Please forgive her because she really wants to do well in her business. Thank you that I love her without it being a burden. And thank you for your total use of us for your glory. I pray that all things work out to your glory. Thank you for Elden. Without him, I would probably never had met her and known the wonder of just how much you suffer from loving us. I repent for every idle act in ignorance I have committed. And thank you so much for staying close by as I struggled with being me. Now I know what heartache I personally gave you. Again, I ask that you give me the wisdom, knowledge, and understanding, coupled with courage, to act speedily on your requests and commands. I love you, Father, and I love you, Jehoshua. Thank you for suffering in a body like mine and maintaining your integrity and faithfulness to Father for us all. Thanks for all who are written on my list and those who are not.

Ellen,

Seeing you yesterday was the highlight of my day! As well as going to see my guardian mom, I went to see if I could stand not seeing you for a length of time. I wanted to come right back. I passed through on Shabbat to see you, but I didn't.

Lady, I am not able to do anything without you on my mind and heart. I cannot sleep right now because I failed to seize the moment and tell you my love for you and only you. I do love the other women, but only you have my heart and soul. I am yours, and I am very happy to be.

You are not like the other women, but you have a propensity to be like them. That is why I am telling you this now. I love you because you are love and a very special woman (lady), and I don't want you to be like them. Vided, my little sister, is an exception. I love her dearly, but only as a sister, and you know how siblings feel about each other.

Please forgive me for not sharing this with you when I was with you. I am a good writer and a thinker but not too good at seizing the moment to speak what I think and feel. And what I feel for you is, really, beyond words. That is why I want to be with you until I die. And if what I think and feel will give us quite a few years together, I will never be a burden to you. But I will care for you and love you, like a young man would. Oh, how I love you!

I am hoping that I will see you after I have had my treatment today. I have the courage to tell you this, and I hope I have the opportunity, and you will be pleased.

Loving you forever,
William

Today I followed my heart and the urging of Father Jehovah, I believe, in telling the most beautiful lady I have met up close that I love her. There was more to say, but that was the most important. All my waking time was spent talking to Father about it, and I was assured that the outcome was on him. He made us both, and it was his love in us for each other. After that, I have had the most marvelous day, with Father giving me very warm greetings from three lovely young ladies at Dairy Queen.

After that, I had a delicious dinner with a former lover: shrimp, vegetables, and a veggie pasta. I had seconds, and I hope it didn't add back an ounce of weight that I have lost.

Tired, I now hope to sleep with pleasant dreams all night.

Thanks, Father, for Ellen and her associates, and bless their business.

I have spent another wonderful and beautiful day in Father's grace. I spent a short time with two other pretty daughters of Father's. They don't have the love for me that Ellen has displayed or the respect. Another Eva has appeared, and Greselle is making innuendo so that I might become involved with her, as what happened with the first. It is apparent to them that if I love a lady, I will do anything good that I can for her.

Dear Ellen,

Tonight, October 14, 2016, I took a prayer walk around the community I reside in with my mother and niece. As I did, Father told me the meaning of a dream and/or vision I had about you a few weeks ago. I did not know what it meant until he told me tonight. I am writing it to myself on WhatsApp so that I won't forget it. I will either let you read it from here or forward it to you.

Father showed me that you have or will have full authority to heal the most impossible ailments and diseases, and I am the recipient of such healing or shall be.

I don't know if you know this about yourself or not. But I repeat, you are awesome! In case you forgot, that was my response to your translation of what you told your associates at dinner at the Cheesecake Factory, which you relayed to me. I later thought it was a stupid response, but now I understand what came through me and also why I feel like I do about you. As our Father is awesome, so are you…in him!

Father Jehovah,

Thank you for the day ended, and this new day began. As always, you have magnified yourself through Messiah Joshua and glorified his name. He glorified your name and taught us how to love and honor you in every aspect of this life, leading to eternity. I thank you for choosing me, delivering me into your kingdom of god and light, and opening doors to your way of righteous living and not my presumed way.

Father, your sons and daughters are handsome and beautiful, and I am overjoyed at some of them from Israel and from around the world. I most especially give thanks for Ellen and the love you have for her in me. I look forward to understanding it to the fullest and to loving you even greater for you are awesome and wonderful, beyond speaking or thinking, by man's mind. I thank you for giving me this measure of grace that allows me to have abundance of life.

Father, I pray for your churches in Messiah Jesus. Please forgive us for not knowing and reading your name where your prophets and writers have written it. Teach us all to love your name and all people. Help us overcome religious hatred and ignorance and embrace love and life in you, through Messiah Joshua.

Amen.

Father just shared with me that if we knew and know Jesus (Jehoshua), then we would know him and his name, as well as his eternal nature. Many know about him through the Scriptures and the preaching and the teaching of some but have not yet met Jesus (Jehoshua). I am an instrument for such introduction.

How can one be one with Father Jehovah when living in a relationship that is unholy? Father requires that we live according to his Holy Spirit and not according to the flesh. The flesh, when not in subjection to the spirit of God, is sinful. Yet the spirit that is within that unholy flesh is redeemable. All spirits within the flesh is redeemable by the sacrifice of Jehovah's son, Jehoshua (Jesus). All that is needed is trust and obedience to the word of Jehovah in him.

When this is the case, the word of Jehovah is sent to the obeying believers, and they are born of that Holy Spirit, and the believers are born Yehovah's children. All things become new, and all sin and its power are canceled. We are brand-new beings in old flesh yet brand-new. If the newborn is in a proper environment his/her growth is rapid and strong. If the environment is not, then the growth is slow and steady and sometimes aborted. This is what Jesus is telling us in his parable of the sower. Religion and denominations within religion is a great problem for us. However, Jesus is with us in the spirit of which we are born. Our hearts and minds (wills) are also environments that prompt our growth or lack thereof. Both Jehovah and Jesus have commanded us to be holy, like Jehovah our God is holy, and to be perfect like our father, Jehovah in heaven is perfect. This holiness and perfection is not of ourselves. It is of Jehovah our God and Father, through Jesus (Yehoshua), his only begotten Son. So they are not telling us to go and become holy and perfect of our own account. They are telling us that this is their gift to us for their glory. Therefore, you're born again in the same flesh and given power over the flesh.

I am experiencing the very thing right now. I joined others to pray for Father's guidance in my love for a beautiful young woman tonight. She is one of the most beautiful and youngest women I have been privileged to see with my natural eyes, if not the most beautiful and the youngest. And I see very well. She knows my love for her, both from me and Father. Of all the pictures of her in her album, she showed me a picture of her in a bikini bathing suit. I saw, but her face and eyes appeal to me more than her body. They are there, and her skin is flawless and beautiful too. My love is for her eternal soul, combined with her body. Of course, the temple in which she is housed plays a great role in my attraction to her. But I must see Jehovah in his Holy Temple (her). He has shown me that very thing. But it is to come. I must also be Jehovah's Holy Temple for me to have a oneness with her in him. Total trust and obedience to his will must be present in both of us if we are going to be equally yoked together, as we are told in the Holy Scripture. Being in the same local congregation and believing that congregation's doctrines or articles of faith do not constitute equally yoked. Otherwise, I would not be available to experience my current state. And divorce would not be a personal experience of mine. People have thrown me away because of it and said that I am a poor minister of Jesus's gospel. Thanks to Jesus and Jehovah, they do not have the final word on my existence.

Although I have this state of being, I am in Father Jehovah and Jesus, holy and perfect. To their glory! I encourage you to accept their gifts to you.

After praying with my brother and sister, I am going along great. That is why I am writing this. We three, plus one other, are cofounders of the Prince of Peace Ministry, which Father is taking worldwide, through the internet and by personal visits soon. You may have noticed that I have been using Father Jehovah's name. It is at his request. He gave it to Moses (Moshe) to share with us and to show proof of his call and for us to know. I am not a part of a denomination that claims exclusively to be his witness. I am just one of his obedient sons who love him with all our heart, soul, mind, and strength. I am here only for him. Though, in ignorance, I did not accept gifts he had and presented for me, those days are over. I love being one with Father, Jesus (Jehoshua), and his family. Therefore, I will not refuse anything or anyone. I may be refused, but I will not be the refuser! Praises to you, Father, and to you, Jesus, for all the blessings you have given and hold in store for the proper time and for your glory. Amen.

Given to me, William W. (D) Weathers this Friday, November 4, 2016.

I Love You with All of Me

I love you with every breath and every thought that I take and have. You tell me that it is crazy for me to think, hope, and feel the way that I do about you. I want to believe what you say and dispel such thought, hope, and feeling, but I just can't. Since you want me but are afraid to accept me for the reason that our relationship is crazy, I have done all that I can to stop it. I call you, and you answer with a text, saying, "Stop!" That I can do. I can stop calling you, but I can't stop wanting to call you, to see you, and to be with you for eternity. I know that after life on Earth, there is no marriage of men and women. Jehoshua told us that, and it is recorded in the New Testament of the Holy Scriptures. However, we are eternal beings wrapped up in mortal skin, supported by flesh, bones, and blood. We existed with Father Jehovah before we came to be in these bodies we inhabit. We will live eternally, after our time in these bodies expire. But the decisions we make while in these bodies determine where and how we spend eternity after we leave these bodies. You and I were meant for each other, and we are sent here to redeem our kind. We are sent in the spirit of our father Jehovah as followers of his son Jehoshua. I did not look for you because I did not know these things until I met you and loved Israel and Israelis as I do. You know my story with the special ladies of Dead Sea Cosmetics. But you don't know the why. I didn't know either until I obeyed Father in prior issues and am now writing this. Eve and Eva are the only two who were special to me, and Eva more than Eve. Eve was twenty-two years old when we met. I love her but only wanted to see her a second time to know that she was real. I have never seen Eve as I saw her that day.

Her photos don't match how I saw her. Eva just used my affection for her to sell me her products, and she did care a little beyond that. But she is not you.

You are unbelievable! You were completely honest with me about your relationship with you boyfriend though I don't know what boyfriend means in your community. I have another from your community who has a boyfriend. But she told me that if I needed some loving, I could see her. I am not a street person, so I don't know what that means, but I felt that it was sexual.

I love and miss you so much that I didn't want to write. But Father insisted, and as I write, he is revealing this to me. I have lived for this moment alone. To meet you, marry you, and fulfill the rest of Father's will for us until we leave these bodies we each live in. And as long as eternity is, our story will inspire others. That is, if you choose to accept his will for us. We already love each other more than we can stand. I have forgotten about the thoughts of man. Because when they could and still can know Father Jehovah, they chose differently. They've chosen a temporary life of pleasure, unspeakable wealth of money; sex with men, women, children, and babies; recreational use of drugs and alcohol; and the perversion of all the things Father put on Earth for our good. So they don't know how to guide and encourage us to do Father's will.

They, by the blinding of Satan, are jealous of those of us who have extraordinary callings from Father. They are afraid that we will be more than they. But Father intends that we all be inheritors of all that is his and that we enjoy our inheritance here on Earth eternally. He is never going to die. He made the Earth to be inherited by us and ruled as he rules in heaven. It was meant forever, but men listened to their enemy, just like most do today.

Of all the women in the world, Father grew love in me for you. There is no other woman on Earth today for me. There are plenty of them here though. I find most to be pleasant to the eyes and are fine to share Father's time and space with. But none are suitable for me. You are the only one. I have told you before that I would not or was not waiting for you to come to me or accept me. I meant it to assure you that I didn't want to put you under pressure to come to me. But it was not the truth. As a matter of fact, I can't live without you. Without you, there is no motivation to wake in the morning. I lack confidence and courage without you. And I don't want anything in this world if I don't have you. Please find in your heart the place that Father has put in you for me. And open the door so that I may come in and so that we can accomplish our goals and Father's goals for us. They are the same, ours and his. This morning, I woke up early and saw a red ring around your Instagram profile photo. I knew it was something you wanted some people to see, and since it was not hidden from me, it was for me to see also. I am not always encouraged by your posts and stories, but I always care about you, and I always want to encourage you to seek your happiness with all of your heart. Of this, I am confident. Your happiest, most joyful days are with me in Father Jehovah's love!

I am William in Wonderland! I am in a constant state of wonder because of the life Father Jehovah is leading me in. All along, when people meet me and learn that I am the only male in a house with seven sisters, they say that I am spoiled. While nothing can be farther from the truth concerning them, I am spoiled. By my Father Jehovah, I am spoiled. How is this so? Of all the people that I have met in this world, I am the only one who is me. That is true of everybody, but I am unique in that I have embraced Father's plan for me, and I have come out of the religious field, except for righteousness.

I remember my youth and Father's presence there. I was never a mischief lad though I associated with mischief lads from the neighborhood. They got into things that I was not allowed to get into. I remember the first girl that I took a liking to. Her name is Daisy Mae Smith, and I have no idea whether she is still alive or not. She is the first female I ever lost my breath for. One evening, late afternoon, she was visiting my family, and we got into a tag match. She tagged me and ran as fast as she could to prevent me from catching her. She was too slow, and as I reached out my hand to tag her, she balled up and fell to the ground. Before I knew anything, I was falling to the ground! Puff! All of the air went out of my lungs, and I was unconscious. I awoke in the arms of my Uncle Berlin, who was shaking me and crying. When consciousness returned, everybody was crying for joy, and they all hugged me.

Today, August 2, 2018, I have the distinct privilege of living a life of love like never before. I love every person on Earth and one woman with the greatest love ever lavished on a woman from one man. And all that I did was to go from my mother's home to a mall in Miami in search of a friend, looking to find out about her health condition and whereabouts. I never saw her again, but I talked to her on the phone. One day, I went by to visit another friend whom I'd meet in another mall closer to my residence. When I met her, she introduced me to this woman that I love like no other. She was beautiful, but not the prettiest woman I've seen. I was told that she spoke several languages, and I was reminded of Jacqueline Kennedy, President Kennedy's wife.

I didn't think anything of her, consciously, because she was introduced as the boss's wife. Time passed, and I longed to see her more and more. In my loneliness, I was writing of my love to another when this love for her overpowered me and has not stopped to this date. It is strong, mature, and constant! I have written to her of my love and my expectations, as Father has shown me. I love her with the purest of hearts among men. It is a heart redressed after purification by Father Jehovah by his begotten Son, Jehoshua. She likes my writings but has issues with some of the revelations therein. I am just loving her and standing in the path. I have no pretenses in my love for her. Today I have loved her in my Father's love and will never defile her. Any other way would not be love. She introduced me to a medium on the internet. That is how I follow and keep in touch with her. It is a strange way, but it is the way she has chosen. Father has given me a steadfast love for her with what we call the patience of Job. I have lived all this time without her, and I can wait until we are together, or I am sleeping with the fathers of our faith.

Your Beauty

While world-famous makeup makes your beauty shine, and you make it look good, it does not overshadow the beauty that Father gave you. And though slightly altered, nothing can hide the light of your soul. Your light arouses the loving light of my soul and makes strong the beat of my heart. Your eyes illumine the way to peace that is beyond comprehension of the simpleminded and promote the wise. Knowing that you are here fills my soul with joy and the desire to live, longing to see you face-to-face once more. Unbelievable joy came into my heart at our meeting, and sad loneliness filled it until you spoke once again. Contentment of seeing your pictures and an occasional text sustain me from day to day. But nothing compares to eye-to-eye contact. Stay love, my dearest friend. Stay love.

I Had a Dream

I had a dream of the love of my life. She was nothing of what I thought she would be, but she was everything I needed to keep me grounded and encouraged.

When I saw her, light radiated from her brighter than the sun. The closer I got to her, the more I was drawn to her, and I could not halt my steps. The first and most impressive attribute that captivated me were her eyes. They looked up on me, pierced my soul, purged it, and made me pure.

Looking into her eyes was like looking into eternity and seeing pure goodness as far as I could see. I was taken throughout existence, and all was unspeakably wonderful.

Those awesome eyes were gently placed on the most beautiful face and arranged in perfect harmony with the nose and mouth. Those beautiful lips were like gloriously colored clouds perfectly placed on her face. The rest of her is just a compliment to her eyes, face, and lips. All of which are only found in heaven.

I did not know what to do, but I was guided by my heart, and I did not what I thought but what a pure heart does. I loved her with all my life and being. Unbelievably, I felt the same love flowing from her to me. Then I awoke. I looked around, and there was no light, no beautiful eyes, no nose, and those beautiful lips were not there at all. Just like the Temptations song, "It was just my imagination running away with me. Oh, my soul! Why can't my imagination be reality?"

W. Dwightel Weathers,
February 11, 2017

I Was Not Dreaming

I was not dreaming after all! I saw the vision of Jehovah's daughter, born and brought into the world just for me in the winter of my life. The light that radiated from her is the light of her soul. She is virtuous and pure. No man's eyes have seen her, nor any man's hand or mind has ever touched her. For she is for me and me alone. She has not the desire for earthly things for as Jehovah's daughter, she is heir to all things temporal and eternal.

Therefore, her mind is on, pleasing me and affirming the way of Jehovah. She does not question whether the Messiah was sent and has come into the world to redeem Israel and the people of the world. She is one with him and knows how to make me one with them.

No imagination can fathom her. It is the revelation of Jehovah, our God and Father, to keep me assured of his plan and goals for me. I awoke from a vision, and the vision is alive in me to encourage faithfulness and speedy obedience. Oh, my soul! Continue your delight in Jehovah, and do his bidding faithfully and swiftly. Alas! My soul exalts in Jehoshua for he is Jehovah's Messiah, and no other is to come. Jehoshua is the way, truth, and life. No one comes to Father Jehovah except by him. And from him comes my beloved, dressed in white and a purple sash around her waist.

W. Dwightel Weathers,
February 11, 2017, 10:06 PM

Billy, I am writing this to you because I am not ready to write to Ellen.

Good morning, my beautiful and beloved! You made my day so awesome that I had to pass on the joy to two others who were not feeling well and were feeling unloved and uncared for. As a result of the joy I passed to them, they wanted to do a facial for me. But since it was not hours since you did my face, I refused and explained that you had just done it. It should have been evident, but they were so overjoyed and appreciative, they didn't notice.

This morning, I looked in the mirror, and my face was glowing. I don't know if it is because of what you did to my face or what you did to my heart. I have told you before that each time I see you, it is like seeing you for the first time. I just wanted to tell you that you are awesome and amazing. I still love you more than I thought I would love any woman again. God made you very special, and I see it every time I see you!

Lovingly yours,
William

A friend of ours reminded me of a song written and sung by Bill Withers, "Ain't No Sunshine When She's Gone." She is the closest person to me who connects us. I remember times before when you pointed out that I had feelings for several others before I met you. You tried to focus my attention and affection on another. Well, I do love her, but I have support from a source far greater than you and me. It is not an easy thing to maintain perspective while battles are going on around and within. But one thing is sure. When I see you, everything is all right. Unless you show displeasure in seeing me. Although you are a very prominent person in bringing sunshine to my life, Father is the ultimate light of my life. Why you are here and have such an amazing effect on me is incomprehensible, at this point. I love you, and I want to love you without restraint. I want it neither from you nor from me. However, only in Father's will and timing. I realize that I am restraining myself by not completing some very important paperwork. I despise myself for this. I must get this done. I know that I will love you throughout eternity because of the way Father loves you and me. His plans are forever. I close this by declaring my complete devotion to you. Others are here for me to keep sanity as I prepare for you. I love you with all my being, and I am yours forever.

The End of the Road!

I have traveled the road of love for many years and miles.

Love was always my quest and pursuit. I started loving real early. And each one that I loved stayed in my heart because it is pure. As I grew older and more intense, Father began to take a more active role. I love many and all, but there is only one. In my youthful adulthood, Father Jehovah sent his prized daughter to me. I thought I was not ready. But my love for her overwhelmed me. Yet we did not embrace Father's joy for us. Regret holds my heart today. By permission, I loved and took three, and they did not last. The love in me remains, but we are apart. Then there came three very lovely daughters from Father's heart. But they were not the one. When declaring my love for one in writing, there arose a fourth. She is the most beautiful ever. I could not resist loving her, and I tried very hard. She fills all my days, even when she is far away. My love for her takes all my being. I have reached the end of my road. No matter what happens between us, there is no more love for any other. Yes, there is love for all, as it should be. But no one else draws me to a level of love like she does. She is the end of the road. Until my last breath, I love her, my end of the road.

Loving on Autopilot

I have loved the most excellent woman to grace my sight and senses so strong and intense that I cannot stop loving her and wanting to behold her loveliness.

Many days I asked Father Jehovah to relieve me from my heartache associated with loving her.

Somehow, I could not fathom her loving me like I love her. However, I did not want to offend him by rejecting his will. It has been ten months since I've met and loved her.

Father showed me her eternal love and beauty, but she often did things to disprove such a nature in her after I told her. After such a show, I asked Father if I could stop loving her so fervently and purely. His answer was always no, explaining that no matter how often and how much we disappointed and hurt him, he could never stop loving us. I know and regret the disappointments and hurt that I caused him.

Now I hear whispers in the air that I can stop loving her and that it is too late. But I have loved so long and strong that I am on autopilot. When one sees her the way that I see her, it is no wonder that I love her with all my being. Father has told me that she loves me more than I love her. I wonder if this, too, has changed. I only know that I love her and cannot stop! If "too late" means that she is married to the one she is with, I must let her go. I really do not want to do that. But Father's law of love is that one not covet what belongs to another. Yet loving her comes naturally and automatically. The desire to see her awakens me each day and drives sleep from me in the night! My hope and prayers are that the whispers are imaginations, and I still have a chance to win her for eternity. Whatever the turnout, my heart and love are on autopilot, and the controls won't release, so I may navigate a course away from her. This, I really don't like to think about.

See Me in the Morning

See me in the morning, and I will stay with you all day long. I will walk with you every step of the way. I will guard your paths and catch you when you slip. I will lift you in my arms and comfort you with my love. Tenderly, I will tell you my dreams with you and my great success with you by my side. See me in the morning, and I will stay with you all the day long. At night, I will cover you, from head to toe, in love and give you peaceful rest. My eyes will not close as I watch you sleep. I will watch the blink of your eyes to the beauty of your dreams or the dread of Leviathan pursuing your soul. I will enter your dream to combat Leviathan and slay him as I am your knight in shining armor. I will restore your dreams in beauty and grace, like those of heaven. I will kiss your brow and smile at the smile it brings you. See me in the morning, and I will love you so well that everyone will be surprised and jealous that you are the only one who has the place you have in my heart and that there is no other like me who would love so completely and satisfy without thought for myself but for you only. When I see you in the morning, I know that my life is heavenly complete!

What I feared and hoped seems to have happened. Yet I will live each moment of each day loving her with a pure heart. Others were afraid for me that this might happen. That they, she, and the one she lives with might hurt my heart. However, their concern and my attempts not to love her could not stop my love. And now that she appears to be his forever, I still cannot stop loving her and wanting to see her. Because I have not seen her face-to-face in months, I both long to see her and dread seeing her. She's the last I want to be in love with like this.

I could be wrong about my premonition about them, and I don't know how I feel about it. There are certainly more women in the world than she, but not even her sister or her friends and associates are like her. I am relieved that she might not be for me, yet concerned that I am in a vacuum somewhere outside reality.

I look at her in her latest internet post, standing in the arm of her mother. Like I said before, there's not one other like her. She's the most important and influential woman and human alive to me. With her or without her, I have a course to finish, and I will do it. What is really your will, Father Jehovah, for the two of us? Is this love in me for her for some other purpose than we being together?

I Have Fallen in Love and I Can't Get Out!

In the spring of my life, I fell into the hands of some who claimed to care for me. They delivered me into the hands of common peoples and the lost, who thought that they were Socrates. Instead, they were pigs wallowing in mud, thinking it was the regenerative minerals in the mud of the Dead Sea. As I was in that mud, I felt my life slipping away. Resolution after resolution, I sank deeper into death. I cried to my father, whom I did not know because of the mud. But he heard my cry. And while still in the spring of my life, he heard me.

All of a sudden, I was falling. Deeper and deeper and deeper into love, I fell. From head to toe, from the crown of my head to the sole of my feet, I was covered. "Hey!" I cried. "What's going on?" No one could give me an answer. Parents had no answer. Siblings had no answer.

Pastor had no answer, and friends had none, but one said, "You're too smart!" What? Too smart? Who can be too smart? Only God can be that smart. "What's wrong with you?" I see everybody differently. Before, I only saw pretty and ugly, but now I see everybody as pretty. Are they beautiful as well? Deeper and deeper into love, I fell. My heart was beating differently from before. My breathing and my hearing, everything is different.

But the people began to ask, "Are you all right? Nobody else has what you have." We see and condemn sin and sinners, even ourselves, because no one can be like you, but God and his begotten Son, Jesus! And you surely are not him. We know you. Confusion, confusion, and more confusion! Why am I the only one? Can't somebody else be wrapped up in love? I love this state of being in love. But it is so lonely. Babies and animals and the very old like my presence, and also the young children. Love is so grand. Even in the loneliest times, love is here to comfort and assure! Love never leaves me alone, and love never breaks my heart, soul, or mind, neither does my spirit! Love makes me stronger and stronger, and love makes me love stronger and stronger!

Love fills the air with music. Sweet, beautiful, melodic music that lasts and lasts. Love does not allow unrequited love to destroy. Love takes love and builds again and again. But there are no walls. If any dares to come close enough, love wraps them from head to toe, from the crown of the head to the sole of the feet. Love does not allow defeat. Love alone destroys every foe, every enemy with love. Love destroys death and everything evil. That is why I have fallen into love, and I cannot get out. Love has destroyed every evil in me and replaced it with everything good. I cannot look upon the bikini-clad beauty and want anything but good for her. And since I am a man, no matter how handsome a male is, I only have love for him. I tell you that I have fallen into love, and I cannot get out. And I really don't want to. Prettiness turns to wrinkles if life remains that long. Money fails when old age, illness, and death come knocking. But love regenerates the ones raptured by its pureness every day. They who are in love will never taste death. For the day they fall into love, death is destroyed for them.

Oh, won't you fall in love with me? There is greatest joy, no deceit, and everything is good and everlasting. Yes! Even the things that are visible have everlasting counterparts that are eternal. I keep falling deeper and deeper in love, and she cannot entice me to come out. I looked ahead and saw that all that she offers leads to misery, shame, and ultimately, death eternal. So I hold out my hand to her in love and ask gently, "Come! Fall in love with me. I assure you, you will never regret it." All riches and all things are owned by love. Won't you fall in love with me? I have fallen in love, and love won't let me go!

About the Author

W. Dwightel Weathers is the only son out of William R. and Emma G. Weathers's eight children. He began writing at an early age and has published two poems in the *Robert Frost Anthology*. He was born in Mississippi and relocated to Miami, Florida, in 1960 with his family.